Help Me Remember the Plagues of Egypt

By Delphine Branon Bates

I'll help you remember!

Illustrated by Delphine Branon Bates and EsDesign

LifeSong Publishers

Somis, CA

ISBN: 978-0-9799116-4-8

Copyright 2010 by LifeSong Publishers

Published by LifeSong Publishers
P.O. Box 183, Somis, CA 93066-0183
805-504-3916
www.lifesongpublishers.com

Scripture quotations are taken from the Holy Bible, New Living Translation, Copyright © 1996. Used by permission of Tyndale House Publishers, Inc., Wheaton, Illinois 60189. All rights reserved.

Artwork and book design by Delphine Branon Bates and EsDesign.
Printed in South Korea

Library of Congress Cataloging-in-Publication Data

Bates, Delphine Branon, 1945-
  Help me remember the Plagues of Egypt / by Delphine Branon Bates ; illustrations by Delphine Branon Bates and EsDesign.
      p. cm. -- (Help me remember series ; 2)
  ISBN 978-0-9799116-4-4 (hardcover)
  1. Moses (Biblical leader)--Juvenile literature. 2. Plagues of Egypt--Juvenile literature. 3. Christian education of children--Activity programs. I. EsDesign (Firm) II. Title.
  BS580.M6B28 2010
  222'.1209505--dc22
                          2010009699

Comments

"If someone were to ask me right now, 'What did God create on the 5th day?' or 'What's the 5th commandment?' or 'What's the 5th plague brought upon by the Egyptians?'...I would know the answer! And I would have Delphine Bates and her wonderfully imaginative books to thank for it. Honestly, she has given us, young and old alike, an ingenuous way to memorize the Ten Commandments, the Seven Days of Creation and, finally, the Ten Plagues of Egypt. What's more, she makes it so easy. You really must have these little treasures in your home and church library."

—Joni Eareckson Tada, Joni and Friends International Disability Center

With unforgettable vivid imagery, Delphine Bates creatively provides wonderfully attractive and interesting resources for aiding kids (adults, too) to indelibly etch key biblical material, like the Seven Days of Creation, the Egyptian Plagues, and the Ten Commandments, on their young minds. Every Christian parent should use these memorable materials with their children.

—Richard Mayhue, Th.D., Dean, The Master's Seminary, Sun Valley, CA

Whether recalling a name, phone number or computer password, we often utilize word-pictures, acrostics, sound-alikes or visualization to help us remember. Amazingly, that's what the three "Help Me Remember" books do. By incorporating unique, creative and effective memory aids, Delphine Bates applies numerous mnemonic devices to tell the story of the character and purposes of God in the Bible. Refined over the years from teaching her own children and grandchildren, she now shares her secrets with us. Researched and accurately portrayed, learners of any age will find themselves easily grasping the central elements of these important parts of biblical history.

—Dr. Irv Busenitz, Vice President for Academic Administration, The Master's Seminary

To my husband, John, and our grandchildren-
JT, Curren, Whitney, Sierra, Tanner, Sheller, McKinley,
Wyatt, Ezra, Jonas, Andee, Silas, Olive, and Wilson.

"Choose today whom you will serve...as for me and my family,
we will serve the LORD." Joshua 24:15

Delphine

The Plagues of Egypt
(partial quotes from the following verses)

Plague 1: Exodus 7:17—"Look! I will hit the water of the Nile with this staff, and the river will turn to blood."

Plague 2: Exodus 8:2—"I will send vast hordes of frogs across your entire land from one border to the other."

Plague 3: Exodus 8:16—"The dust will turn into swarms of gnats* throughout the land of Egypt."   (*also called lice or ticks)

Plague 4: Exodus 8:21—"I will send swarms of flies throughout Egypt."

Plague 5: Exodus 9:3—"The Lord will send a deadly plague to destroy your horses, donkeys, camels, cattle, and sheep."

Plague 6: Exodus 9:10—As Pharaoh watched, Moses tossed the soot into the air, and terrible boils broke out on the people and animals throughout Egypt.

Plague 7: Exodus 9:23—The Lord sent a tremendous hail storm against all the land of Egypt.

Plague 8:   Exodus 10:4—"I will cover the whole country with locusts."

Plague 9:   Exodus 10:21—Then the Lord said to Moses, "Lift your hand toward heaven, and a deep and terrifying darkness will descend on the land of Egypt."

Plague 10: Exodus 12:12—"On that night I will pass through the land of Egypt and kill all the firstborn sons and firstborn male animals in the land of Egypt."

Be sure to read the whole story of the Plagues of Egypt in Exodus 7-12.

The First Plague

This one drop of blood helps us remember how Moses touched the Nile River with his staff and the river turned to blood.

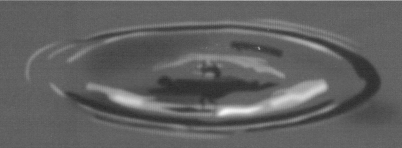

Can you find a number 1 in this picture?

And can you find one of
anything in the picture?

"Look! I will hit the water of the Nile with this
staff, and the river will turn to blood."
—from Exodus 7:17—

The Second Plague

Frogs were everywhere!
This frog is looking for his friends...
thousands of his friends.

Can you find a number 2 in this picture?

And can you find two of
anything in the picture?

*"I will send vast hordes of frogs across
your entire land from one border to the other."*
—from Exodus 8:2—

The Third Plague

Gnats swarmed throughout Egypt.
Gnats, gnats, everywhere!

Can you find a number 3 in the picture?

And can you find three of anything in the picture?

"The dust will turn into swarms of gnats throughout the land of Egypt."
—from Exodus 8:16—

The Fourth Plague

And then... bothersome, buzzing flies!
Meet Buzz, Buzz, Buzz, and Buzz.

Missed 'em!

Can you find a number 4 in this picture?

And can you find four of
anything in the picture?

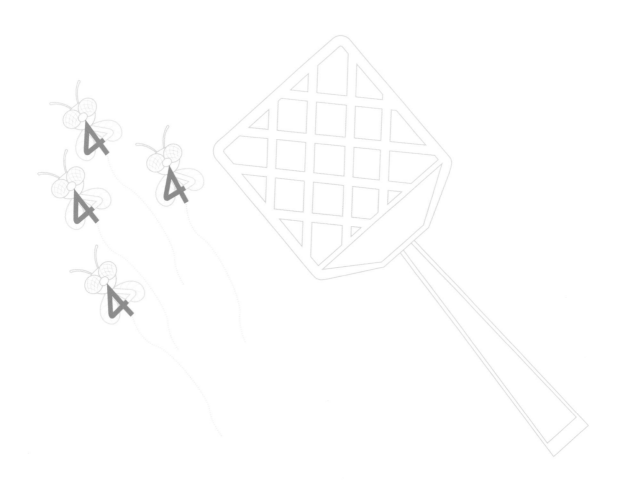

"I will send swarms of flies throughout Egypt."
—from Exodus 8:21—

The Fifth Plague

Next came the animal plague. This deadly disease destroyed the Egyptians' animals that were in their fields.

Can you find a number 5 in this picture?

And can you find five of anything in the picture?

"The Lord will send a deadly plague to destroy your horses, donkeys, camels, cattle, and sheep."
—from Exodus 9:3—

The Sixth Plague

Boils!
The Egyptians and their animals
had sores all over their bodies.

Can you find a number 6 in this picture?

And can you find six of
anything in the picture?

*As Pharaoh watched, Moses tossed the soot
into the air, and terrible boils broke out on the
people and animals throughout Egypt.
—from Exodus 9:10—*

The Seventh Plague

Hailstones struck the people and animals left
out in the fields. They hit every plant
and shattered every tree.

Can you find a number 7 in this picture?

And can you find seven of anything in the picture?

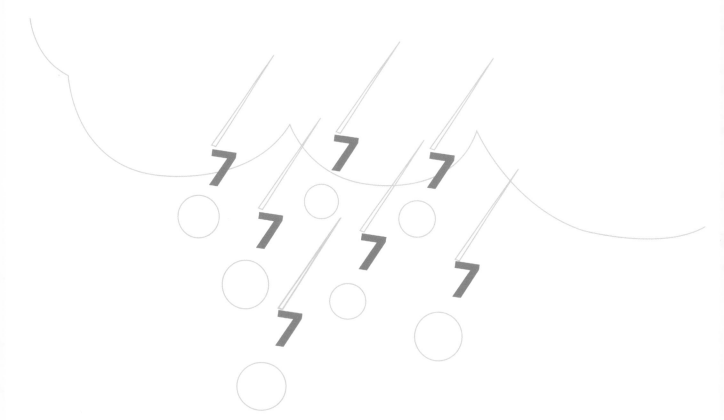

The Lord sent a tremendous hail storm against all the land of Egypt.
—from Exodus 9:23—

The Eighth Plague

A swarm of locusts invaded Egypt.
This fat bug reminds us that insects
devoured the crops and trees.

Can you find a number 8 in this picture?

And can you find eight of
anything in the picture?

"I will cover the whole country with locusts."
—from Exodus 10:4—

The Ninth Plague

There was scary, black darkness over the land.
The darkness was like a cloudy night
when a flashlight is turned off.

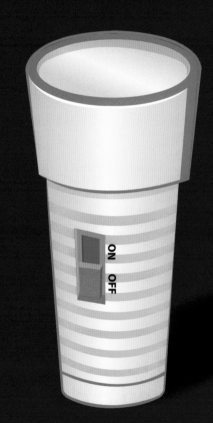

Can you find a number 9 in this picture?

And can you find nine of
anything in the picture?

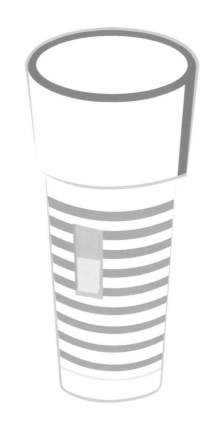

**Then the Lord said to Moses, "Lift your hand toward heaven, and a deep and terrifying darkness will descend on the land of Egypt."
—from Exodus 10:21—**

The Tenth Plague

The last plague brought the death of all the firstborn sons and firstborn male animals in Egypt.

Can you find a number 10 in this picture?

And can you find ten of anything in the picture?

"On that night I will pass through the land of Egypt and kill all the firstborn sons and firstborn male animals in the land of Egypt."
—from Exodus 12:12—

He performed miraculous
signs and wonders in Egypt;
Pharaoh and all his people watched.

— Psalm 135:9—

Thank you to everyone who has shared their
ideas over the years, answered my
theological questions, or cheered me on.
And, most importantly, to the One who even the wind
and waves obey... my Savior.

May I help you remember who He is?
John 20:31

More Help Me Remember Books

Help Me Remember the Days of Creation
by Delphine Bates

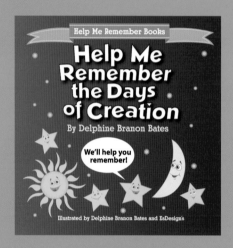

Help Me Remember the Ten Commandments
by Delphine Bates

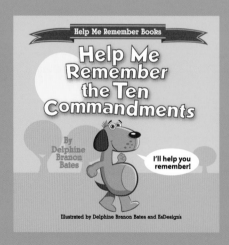

More LifeSong Books

Mr. Blue—A Job For You
by Laurie Donahue and Bryan Hintz
(with cut-out pieces for puzzle and play)

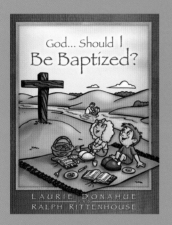

God...Should I Be Baptized?
by Laurie Donahue and Ralph Rittenhouse
(workbook for 8-12 years of age)

The Lord's Supper...Let's Get Ready!
by Laurie Donahue and Paul Phillipps
(workbook for 8-12 years of age)

Find these plus Bible Studies and
other books for adults at:
www.LifeSongPublishers.com
(or your favorite bookstore)
805-504-3916

Egyptian Plagues Counting Challenge

Answer Key
(you may find more than what is listed here)

Plague One: 1 large drop of blood, 1 small drop of blood, 1 puddle of blood

Plague Two: 2 eyes, 2 eyebrows, 2 front feet, 2 knees, 2 back legs, 2 front legs

Plague Three: 3 flowers, 3 gnats left behind, 3 rocks, 3 plant leaves

Plague Four: 4 flies, 4 fly noses, 4 trails behind flies

Plague Five: 5 eyelashes on each eye, 5 whiskers behind ears, 5 markings on each horn

Plague Six: 6 circles on collar, 6 points on collar

Plague Seven: 7 hailstones, 7 hailstone trails

Plague Eight: 8 blades of grass, 8 light blue squares on scarf, 8 veins on leaf, 8 bug fingers

Plague Nine: 9 gold stripes on flashlight

Plague Ten: 10 sheep, 10 toes, 10 tufts of wool on top of heads, 10 noses on sheep, 10 stripes on tunic